Survival Skills

You Cannot Live Without

Prepping and Survival Series

M. Usman

Mendon Cottage Books

JD-Biz Publishing

Disclaimer

The information is this book is provided for informational purposes only. It is not intended to be used and medical advice or a substitute for proper medical treatment by a qualified health care provider. The information is believed to be accurate as presented based on research by the author.

The contents have not been evaluated by the U.S. Food and Drug Administration or any other Government or Health Organization and the contents in this book are not to be used to treat cure or prevent disease.

The author or publisher is not responsible for the use or safety of any diet, procedure, or treatment mentioned in this book. The author or publisher is not responsible for errors or omissions that may exist.

Warning

The Book is for informational purposes only and before taking on any diet, treatment, or medical procedure, it is recommended to consult with your primary health care provider.

Our books are available at

1. Amazon.com
2. Barnes and Noble
3. Itunes
4. Kobo
5. Smashwords
6. Google Play Books

Table of Contents

Preface...4

Building a Shelter...5

Finding Water and Food 9

Defending Yourself...12

Signaling for Help...15

Know How to Start a Fire 18

Finding Your Direction...21

Learn Basic First Aid..24

Have the Right Attitude 27

Practicing Good Hygiene 30

Conclusion 33

Author Bio...34

Publisher..45

Preface

Have you ever imagined what you would do if a boat you were traveling in started sinking? And think of what would happen when traveling in a desert and your car suddenly breaks down with no help around? Knowing just the essential survival skills could define your chances of living to tell your tale another day. Otherwise, you could be doomed.

You might think someone would possibly come your way to save you. But remember, luck is no different from having your life hanging by a rotten thread. Of course, help may come, but sometimes, way too late.

People who make it out of a survival situation are driven by something every time – to see their kids or wife again, etc. But no matter how hard you might try, if you do not know what it takes to survive times like these, you will realize how mean Mother Nature can be.

In this book, you will discover the most important survival skills you must know. It does not matter who you are or what you do, we are all equally in danger of finding ourselves in situations that might force us out of our comfort zone.

Enjoy the reading!

Building a Shelter

Did you know that in extreme conditions, you can only live for up to 3 hours without shelter? If you think that is scary, you are right, and it is the reason we all need to have this survival skill up our sleeve. A good shelter will keep you warm when it's cold and dry when it rains.

The best part is that you do not need a license or years of experience to build one of these. Forget about foundations, windows, and everything you believe a house should have. You are not trying to impress anyone – your goal is to get home in one piece. So, the shelter should be simple, but at the same time, effective.

Choosing a Location

Before you can start your building project, you will need to choose a good location. You might spend time and energy building a perfect shelter, but if location is overlooked, you might regret it. Here are some things to consider:

- ***Think of Wind***: Open areas do not make good locations for a shelter. Unlike houses built by trained builders, your shelter will have no significant reinforcement. Therefore, it could easily be destroyed by wind, leaving you with nowhere to run. Choose an area that is surrounded by trees, rocks, or anything that can slow down the wind.

- ***Avoid Riverbeds***: You might be tempted into building near a river for easier access to water. But in the case of heavy rains, you could easily find yourself caught in a flash flood.

- ***Choose Close To Necessities***: Although you should avoid riverbeds, do not go too far away from a source of water, food, or firewood. Otherwise, you will lose the little energy you have left trying to get these.

- ***Go For Dry Areas***: A wet ground will make you feel cold which is counterproductive.

- ***Don't Build Near Dead Trees***: These could fall on you while you are asleep. The same can be said for rocks that appear to be loose and are big enough to destroy your shelter.

- ***Easy to Find***: Since people will be looking for you, build where rescuers will easily find you.

- *Avoid Caves*: Remember animals have no hands, which makes building a shelter for themselves impossible. So a cave is their favorite place.

How to Build a Shelter

While there a lot of ways to build a shelter when caught in a survival situation, this chapter will only focus on the easiest and most effective. This shelter does not need any special materials, making it feasible for nearly any environment. Building it is easy, but it is gathering materials (debris) that takes time. Here is how you do it:

1. Find a pole that is strong. It should be longer than your height with you arms raised.

2. Find support – a tree fork is the best example of this. If you cannot find it, any structure sturdy enough to hold your pole in place will do. One end of the pole should be on the ground and the other should rest on your support, preferably, not higher than your hip height. When done, it should form a structure resembling a triangle.

3. Gather branches for ribbing. These should rest on the pole on both sides. You might need to keep them compact to prevent debris from getting into your house.

4. Gather debris (dry leaves) - a minimum of 2 feet is recommended. But if it is extremely cold, you will need more. This should be put on the ribs.

5. Gather more branches to keep the debris from being blown away by wind.

6. Make a bed of leaves inside your shelter. This will keep your body

heat from escaping into the ground. It should be at least 8 inches from the ground.

7. Since your new shelter may house some bugs that will give you a hell of a time when you go to sleep, smoke it to get rid of these.

Finding Water and Food

When lost, be it in a desert, jungle, or anywhere, one of the most important things needed to keep you alive is water. Under normal conditions, an adult will live for 2 – 4 weeks without food. But try the same without water, and you only have a maximum of 3 days. Actually, you will be feeling like you were hit by a train on the second day.

Water

If you are lost in a jungle, your chances of finding water are good, than say, if you are in a desert. However, you should never wait till you are thirsty to start looking for water. Dehydration is dangerous and could lead to death in a matter of days. If you notice you are thirsty, feel weak, and most importantly, have dark colored urine, you are already dehydrated.

Here are some tips for finding water:

- **Follow Animals**: Animals cannot live without water. Even though they can walk long distances without it, they still need it from time to time. So, they will always live near a water source. If you can follow them at dawn, they will likely lead you to water. Insects are also a good indication.

- **Green Vegetation**: Anywhere you will see vegetation means there is water nearby. You can try digging a hole and wait for water to collect in it.

- **Low Areas**: Water flows from highlands to lowlands. If you have a map, let this guide you. Alternately, you can get on the highest land in the area and look for any low-lying places. If there is some vegetation, that is where you should be heading (having a binoculars will help).

- **Dew**: An easy way of finding water is to collect dew from grass and other plants in the morning.

- **Plant Condensation**: If you have a plastic bag, tie it at the end of a tree branch with some leaves inside. Water from transpiration will be collected in the bag. You will need several of these to have enough water.

- **Drinking Urine**: This is not recommended, as urine has dangerous wastes your body just tried to get rid of. However, drinking it would be an alternative if you have nothing else (and I mean nothing else). But know that you cannot do this for long, as it will only lead to more problems.

- *Seawater*: Same as with urine, you are not supposed to drink this. It has a lot of salt capable of destroying your internal organs. And that will transform your situation from bad to worse.

But all those ways of finding water are just the tip of the iceberg. Once you have it, you should filter it. Most importantly, you should boil it, as it could have parasites capable of killing you. So that means you will also need to learn how to start a fire.

Food

Like stated earlier, this is not all that important. But, simply eating something can boost your morale, as most of us wrongly believe we cannot live nor do anything without food. However, some foods could be poisonous so exercise caution.

- *Plants*: If you know the area really well, finding some plants you know are safe to eat should not be that hard. If you are not sure about a certain plant, look for something else. Remember that you can live without food.

- *Fish*: If there is a river nearby, fish should be your best bet. But that means you will need to know some ways of catching it in advance. For example, with a spear, net, etc.

Other things you can eat include insects, bird eggs, snakes, rabbits, turtles, and crabs.

Defending Yourself

You would be sorry to think the only danger when stuck outdoors is lack of water, food, or extreme weather. Depending on where you are, snakes, bears, hippos, and a whole lot of other animals will try to get a piece of you, if given a chance. While there is no foolproof way of protecting yourself when faced with dangerous animals, there are things you can do.

Wild animals have brains of their own and it is difficult, if not impossible, to know what their next move will be. This is what makes dealing with them a bit dangerous. This chapter will give you some tips that might save you in times like these. Although you should also be afraid of humans, the majority will try to help.

Have a Weapon

The best way of defending yourself is to have a weapon of some sort. However, if you are devoid of the proper skills in using it, it will not make any difference. It then does not hurt to invest some time learning how to shoot a gun, bow, use a knife, etc.

Adding to that, you should learn to make weapons using available material, for example, a spear.

When Face to Face with a Wild Animal

In most situations, the majority of animals have no intentions of hurting you. For instance, a snake will try to escape your presence and will only bite if it feels threatened. You are too big to be seen as food (to pythons and other large snakes maybe).

It is the bigger animals you should be scared of. You can think of bears, mountain lions, wolves, etc. The good thing is that with some strategy, you can still make it out in one piece.

Here is what you should remember:

- *Do Not Run*: Running will trigger the animal's instinct that you are prey. Instead, face it and back away slowly.

- *Look Big*: Almost all animals know it is a bad idea to mess with something bigger than it is. So, the bigger and taller you are, the better. You can try spreading your arms to achieve this. There are people who have survived a potential attack simply by using this technique

- *Make Noise*: If it makes a lot of noise, it is probably very dangerous – that is how stupid some animals are. So scream, sing, bang pots, and do anything to drive it away. Do not get carried away though, pay attention to how it is responding to this.

- **Keep Distance**: This is your best friend when faced with a wild animal. It will be reluctant to mount an attack if there is some distance. Not only that, but you will be able to respond better if it decides to charge.

- **Climb a tree**: If you know the animal cannot climb a tree, then you have all the good reasons to seek refuge in one.

- **Avoid Attacking First**: Some animals will attack if you threaten them. Unless it is a gun or something that will take out the beast for good, do not be the one to start the fight. Otherwise, you will give it a license to retaliate. And for your information, they live by fighting for food, mates, and shelter, which makes them good fighters, naturally.

- **Making Eye Contact**: This works, depending on the type animal you are dealing with. Some will take it as a challenge, so they will attack. On the other hand, others will see it as submission and walk away. Making it even more confusing, avoiding eye contact will be seen as fear by other animals. Knowing a little about animal behavior will help.

Signaling for Help

Imagine being lost in the jungle all by yourself. You might have your cellphone, but it is rare to have coverage in these kinds of areas. So in this case, your only hope is to find your way back. But what if you are injured or are simply not sure which way to go? In a situation like this, shelter, water, and fire are the things you need most, as you wait for help to come your way.

However, if you do not know how to alert rescuers of your location, your chances of surviving are very slim. Not to say it will only take luck to be found. So it makes sense to master a few techniques of signaling for help.

Each one of these methods will be effective depending on your conditions and the terrain. Here are the techniques:

- **Fire**: At night, when the skies are clear, starting three fires that form a triangle or a straight line is internationally known as a way of someone calling for help. The fires are supposed to be visible from afar and they should be 25 to 30 meters apart. Be sure they are away from other trees as you can easily start a forest fire.

- **Smoke**: In daylight, smoke is one of the best ways of letting people know of your presence. But this only works when it is calm - forget it if it is raining, windy, etc. For better visibility, make sure the smoke and the background differ. Green leaves and other vegetation will work best in a darker background because they produce white smoke. On the other hand, rubber and other oily substances create black smoke which works with lighter backgrounds.

- **Mirror**: Another simple technique that is effective during daylight is reflecting the sun at your target with a mirror. But it takes a couple of trials to master this skill, so work at it now. Mirrors can be seen up to 100 miles away. Alternatively, any shiny object can be substituted for a mirror, e.g. belt buckle, knife blade, canteen cup, etc.

- **Whistle**: If you have a whistle with you, blowing it three times will also let those who hear it know that you are looking for help.

- **Flashlight**: Learning how to send an S.O.S with a flashlight will be very beneficial. Making it even better, it is very simple – just 3 short, 3 long, and 3 short signals, then pause. Then you can repeat.

- **Improvise**: Even when you have nothing else with you, you can figure out ways of letting people know that you need rescuing. You might try writing in the ground words like "HELP." It is not the most effective technique, but may still work - just make sure it is visible from above.

Know How to Start a Fire

Many underestimate the value of a fire. For the majority of us, our definition probably consists of images of grannies sitting around a fire singing to their grandchildren. But frankly, this is nothing short of an understatement. As a matter of fact, fire is among the three most important things you need for survival, along with shelter and water as the others.

It is shocking to see how many people do not know how to light a fire properly. Considering how important this skill is, it is vital that you take your time to master it.

Before we go into the basics of lighting a fire, here are some reasons it is so important.

- *Keeping Warm*: Even though shelter will keep you safe from extreme weather, complementing it with fire is a good idea. Otherwise, you risk suffering from hypothermia.

- *Providing Light*: Humans do not have night vision, so being in the dark while in a survival situation only makes matters worse. Imagine not seeing what you are drinking or what is behind your back?

- *Purifying Water*: With water being one of the most important things needed to live, boiling your water will ensure that it is safe for drinking. Try consuming it unpurified, and you will open a can of worms

- *Keeping Insects Away*: If you have ever been caught outdoors, then you are well aware of how irritating insects can be. But with smoke from a fire, you will not have to worry much about these.

- *Keeping Away Animals*: This does not always work every time, but to some degree, a fire will keep some dangerous animals away.

- *Cooking Food*: Eating raw food is never recommended. So if you do not have a fire, you are doomed.

Although there are other reasons you might need a fire, these few should make you realize how important it is.

Tips for Starting a Fire

There are a lot of ways to start a fire. Some of the popular ones include with matches, lighter, flint and steel, magnifying glass, batteries and steel wool, and many other methods. It is recommended that you learn a couple of these before you are actually caught in a survival situation.

No amount of reading will teach will teach you how to start a fire. This is something you perfect by getting your hands dirty.

With that, let's look at some basics of starting a fire.

- *Choose a Good Location*: If your site is too windy, you will have a hell of a time starting a fire. Not only that, if it is too far from a fuel source, you will lose the precious energy you should be saving.

- *Clear the Ground*: Fire likes to grow and if the area is not cleared, you will end up with more than you can handle. This is especially true in forests.

- *Gather Materials*: For every fire, you will need tinder, kindling, and fuel. Tinder is any material that easily catches fire (dry leaves, grass). Kindling is relatively easy to ignite so it comes after tinder. Fuel refers to large pieces of wood that come last and ensure that the fire burns longer. The rule is to gather twice as much as you think you will need.

Since you can never know when you will be stuck in a survival situation, always have a lighter or matches wherever you go.

Finding Your Direction

There are stories of people who lost their lives for wasting their available resources by going the wrong way. Without much effort, you can tell that a human's sense of direction is not the best in the world. Ants can march for miles in a straight line. But, try blindfolding a human and he will be walking in circles. That does not mean animals are better than we are – they can win the battle, but they will never win the war, because we are so creative.

We can use the resources around us to find our direction. So, let's talk about being lost in the woods without a compass. Do not panic. Here is what you can do:

Use Shadows

By far, this is the easiest and most reliable way of finding your direction no matter where you are. All you need is the sun. Here are the steps to follow.

1.   Find a stick, about 3 feet long, and plant it in the ground. Make sure the surface is level and there are no obstructions.

2.   Mark the shadow's tip with a stone or anything available.

3.   Wait for 10 to 15 minutes. The shadow will move by a considerable distance.

4.   Mark the new tip of the shadow with whatever tool you used in the other step.

5.   Draw a straight line between the two markings. You will have a west-east line. The first marking is always west no matter where you are or the time. So that means the second is east.

6.   Stand with your left hand on the west side and you will be facing north. That means south is right behind you.

Using a Watch

This is also very easy as long as you understand what is involved. You will need a watch with hands. If yours is digital, simply draw an analog one on a piece of paper with the correct time. Your watch should be in local time.

When in the Northern Hemisphere:

1.   Hold the watch horizontally with the hour clock pointed at the sun.

2.   Bisect the angle between the 12 o'clock mark and the hour hand. The bisecting line will point south.

When in the Southern hemisphere:

1.   Hold the watch horizontally in your hands and point the 12:00 o'clock mark at the sun.

2.   Bisect the angle between the hour hand and the 12:00 mark. The bisecting line will indicate north.

Using Stars

Did you know that there are landmarks in the sky you can use to find your way? Here is how to do it:

In the Northern Hemisphere

• You will need to learn how to find the Big Dipper first. It is visible every night, but changes position depending on where you are and the time of the year. All you do then is identify the North Star and imagine a perpendicular line running down to earth. What you will be looking at in the end is the North Pole.

In the Southern Hemisphere

• You will use the Southern Cross Constellation. It is in a shape of a kite and its two pointer stars form an axis that roughly points to the South Pole. Imagine the axis extending five times the distance between the two pointer stars and you will have south.

Learn Basic First Aid

There are a number of circumstances that could put you in a survival situation. Imagine an earthquake hitting your neighborhood, and, for some reason, taking days for help to come. Or it could be a war that could drive you into the wilderness. Regardless of the situation, we have to realize that danger can come at any time and when we least expect it. And in almost all cases, injuries are never absent.

It could be you or someone in need of medical help. But that does not mean you should begin studying to become a doctor. Just knowing the basics of first aid could be all it takes to save a life.

A good starting point would be Cardiopulmonary Resuscitation (CPR). This is something everyone should know, as it can be used in a range of cases. You can even take the course online for free.

Below are some tips to help someone who has been injured. However, these should not be substituted for professional medical help. Actually, you should seek professional help as soon as you can, regardless of the fact that you have administered some basic first aid.

- **Check Breathing**: With only seconds without breath, a person can check out. If not, other organs can be damaged as a result. So your top priority should be to restore breathing. But, that means you will first need to check for any signs of breath. If you confirm there is none, tilt the head and ensure that there is nothing blocking the airway (do this with the victim lying on their back). After that, you can try mouth to mouth.

- **Do Not Move The Person**: If you suspect the victim has broken their bones, it is not recommended to move them. For all you know, their spine or head could have been damaged in the process and moving them will only make the condition worse. So, make it a habit to check the severity of their injuries first. If there are minor ones, you can carefully move them.

- **Stop Bleeding**: Losing a lot of blood can lead to shock and, in some cases, death. That is why you should always try to stop bleeding as soon as you can. This largely depends on the type of the injury. For small cuts, a cloth or bandage will do. Additionally, letting the victim lie on their back and raise the affected part also helps slow down the bleeding. If you believe the patient is bleeding internally, get medical help.

- ***Give Assurance to the Victim***: You should control your nerves so the victim can feel calm. No matter what the situation, keep assuring them that they will be fine.

As you can see, there is a lot you can learn about first aid. No matter who you are, you should seriously consider in investing in some first aid courses. For a start, you can try volunteering for Red Cross – you will get some basic first aid classes. Adding to this, there is a lot of free material on the internet that will also help you master this.

Have the Right Attitude

It is fascinating to see an average man live for days in the wilderness when someone more physically fit, with enough resources, gives up to nature in the same environment. Ask any survival expert, and they will tell you that if you are devoid of the will to survive, you will dig your own grave.

Some call it attitude and others refer to it as maintaining positivity under hopeless conditions. Whatever the description, this is the cement that keeps all the survival skills and resources in one piece.

If you do not have the attitude, it can be hard to make sound decisions. Fear, loneliness, hopelessness, anger, and many other factors all contribute to this problem. It does not matter how many times you have practiced building a survival shelter, this skill can fly out of your ear in an instant.

You should realize that the brain is the most important tool you need for survival. So, if you let it get clogged with the wrong attitude, you will easily transform your problem from a pond into an ocean.

The moment you realize that you are in a survival situation, S.T.O.P (stop, think, observe, plan).

- *Stop*: Unless there is an immediate danger, sit down, relax, and breathe. The mere thought of realizing that you have a problem at your hand will send the brain into overdrive. And that, will lead to wrong decisions. If you have water, drink some. Act like everything is normal. You will avoid panic and fear.

- *Think*: This means you should look at your options. Do you believe help will come any time soon? If you were to go back, will you be able to find your way? You can ask yourself a number of questions depending on your situation.

- *Observe*: Do you see some form of civilization in the distance? Will it be dark soon, and do you will need shelter and fire? What resources do you have to help you stay alive? These are the type of questions you should be considering.

- *Plan*: Now that you have everything clearly evaluated, it is time to make strategies. If it is getting dark, perhaps you should build a shelter. If you believe people are looking for you, make it easy for them by signaling. The plan you make will depend on your situation, and this is just an example.

Other things to remember

1. No matter where you are going, always let someone know. Additionally, tell them when you will be back.

2. Always carry the basics needed for survival, like water, a first aid kit, etc.

3. Take someone along with you. You will have a higher chance of surviving when not alone

4. Control your fears when you realize you are lost. It is normal to fear, but do not let it control you.

5. Make it a point to do all it takes to survive and get back home. For instance, think of how hard it will be for your kids without you. That will motivate you to do all it takes to stay alive.

Practicing Good Hygiene

Being in the wilderness does not mean you should lose all the hygiene practices you have known for years. Otherwise, you will come out looking like you died 45 years ago. Not only that, but you will also expose yourself to infections that could actually kill you.

The fact that you may not have soap or toothpaste does not mean it's all over. There are a lot of resources out there you can tap.

Call of Nature

Being what it is, you will do what you have to do. If you have no toilet paper, you can use leaves. Just make sure there are soft. A good example is mullein leaves. Alternatively, part the cheeks with your hands and it will come out without messing the sides, so you will have no need to clean. If there is water available, you can use that as well.

Teeth and Mouth

Since you will be eating little to no sugary foods in the wilderness, you should not worry much about cleaning your mouth (unless you have toothpaste and a toothbrush). But if you feel you could use one, you can make a chewing stick. Ashes from wood can be used as toothpaste.

Bathing

Although humans can live for days without a bath, there is no excuse to forgo one if you get the chance. This might be with water from a river, lake, etc. If water is not available, you can try air bathing. Simply remove your clothes and stand in the sun for about an hour.

When bathing, you should focus on the feet, armpits, hands, and crotch. These are the areas known for housing a lot of bacteria and fungus. And before you touch food, always wash your hands if water is available.

Women should also take considerable care to wash their area during menstruation. Otherwise, bacteria and fungus can easily find its way into the urethra.

Wounds

Open wounds provide a simple gateway into the body to harmful organisms. That is why you should avoid using just anything to dress your wounds. And before attending to your injuries, wash your hands. If you have a fire, you can boil some water to use in washing your wounds.

It is also possible to get blisters when in the wilderness. Although painful, you should resist from busting them as they will act as any wound and provide an opening into your body.

Conclusion

You might never know when fate will put you in a survival situation. But if you have all the skills, like those in this book, you will increase your chances significantly. However, you should practice them from time to time. They will become second nature and keep you from panicking in the heat of the moment.

Out of all the survival skills in this book, you should prioritize shelter, water, and fire. At the same time, remember to control your attitude. Fear of being lost should not keep you from exploring the world. Have your survival skills perfected, and you will be fine.

Thank you for reading!

Author Bio

Muhammad Usman is a distinguished medical graduate of Allama Iqbal medical college (AIMC). He is a professional writer who has been in the field for more than 4 years. During this time he has produced 10,000+ articles, blogs, and eBooks on various niches related to diseases, health, fitness, nutrition, and well-being. He is a regular contributor to several journals related to medicine and surgery. He is the editor of several journals and newspapers.

Check out some of the other JD-Biz Publishing books

<u>Gardening Series on Amazon</u>

Health Learning Series

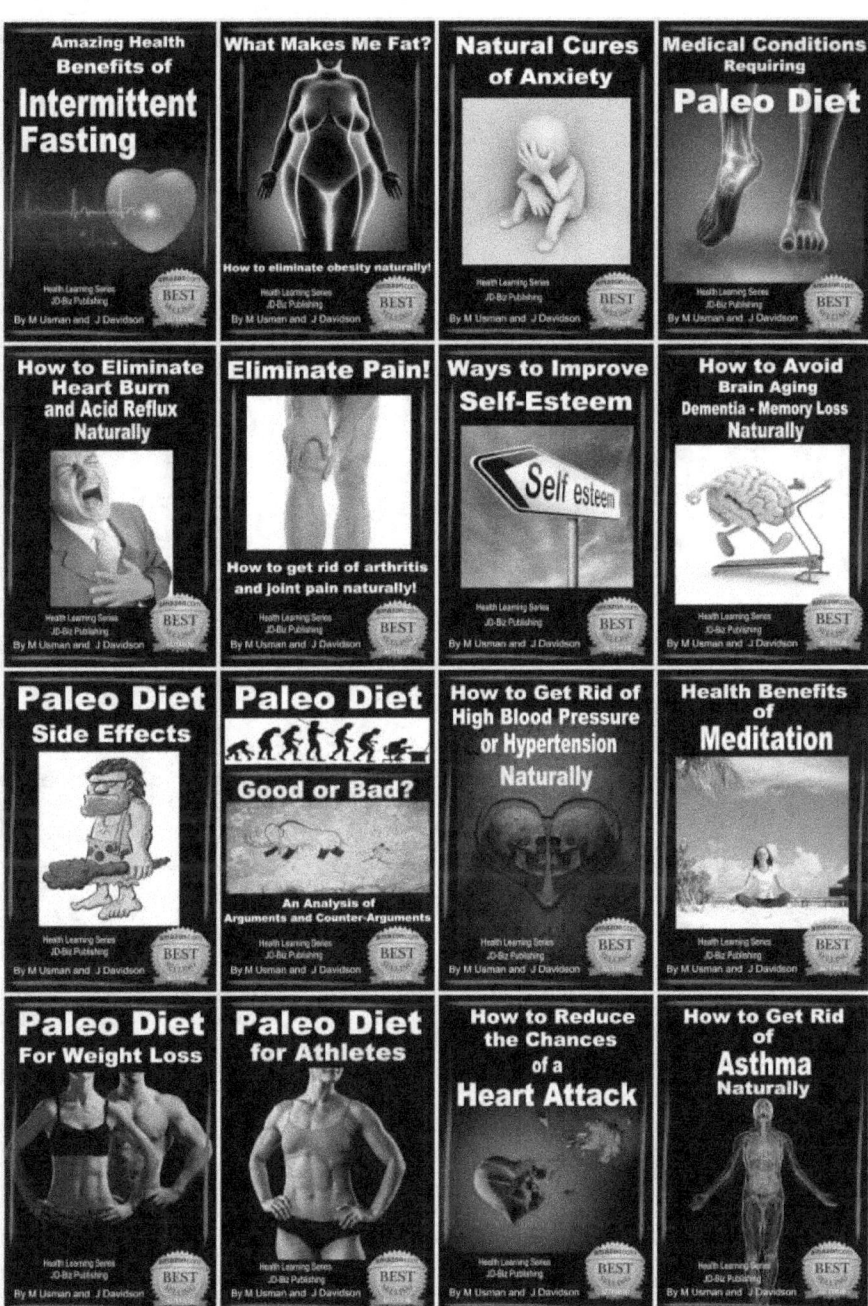

Amazing Animal Book Series

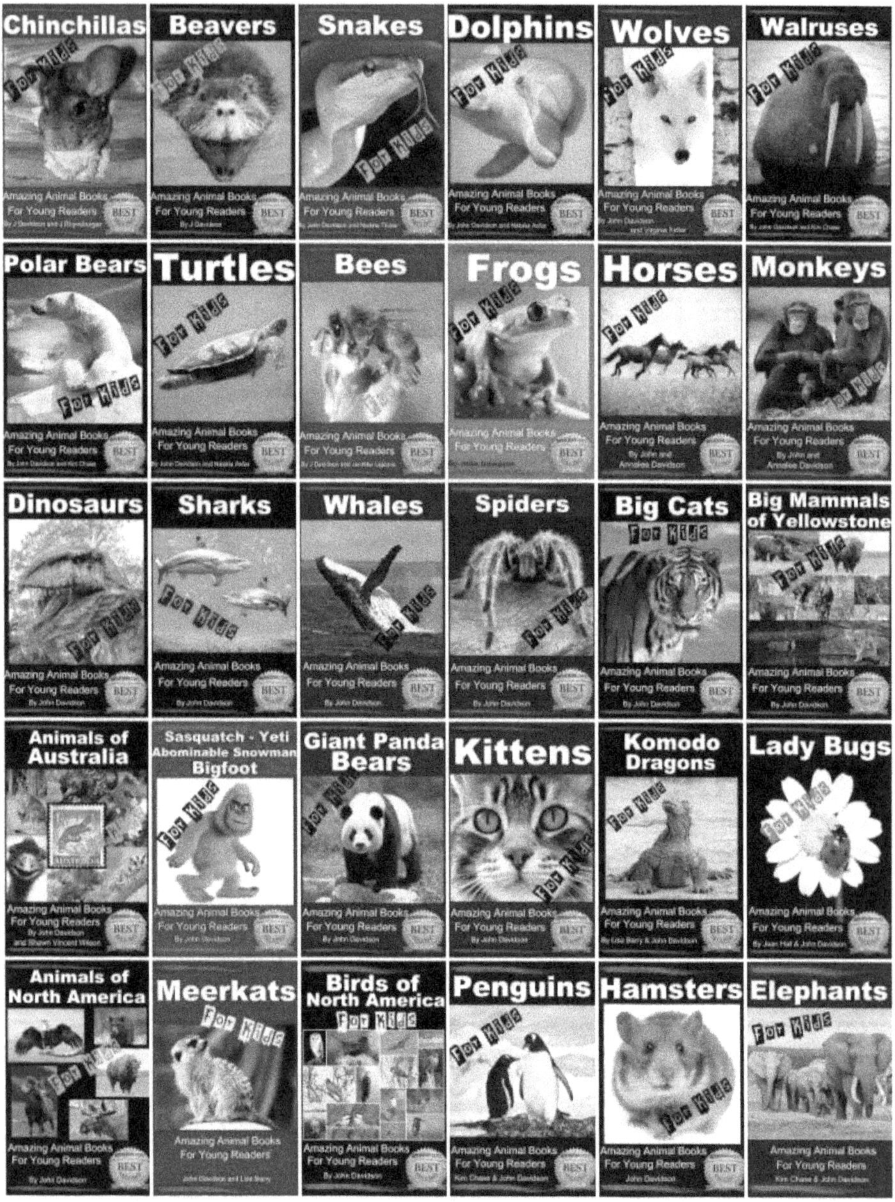

Learn To Draw Series

How to Build and Plan Books

Entrepreneur Book Series

Our books are available at

1. Amazon.com

2. Barnes and Noble

3. Itunes

4. Kobo

5. Smashwords

6. Google Play Books

Publisher

JD-Biz Corp

P O Box 374

Mendon, Utah 84325

http://www.jd-biz.com/

www.ingramcontent.com/pod-product-compliance
Lightning Source LLC
Chambersburg PA
CBHW070344290526
45791CB00003B/1472